THREE BELL ZERO

THREE BELL ZERO
Miles Champion

ROOF BOOKS
NEW YORK

ISBN: 0-937804-82-7
Library of Congress Catalog Card No.: 00-101560

Author photograph by Emma Summerton.
Cover art "Study for Black and White Squares in Squares Painting"
by Peter Davies.

Some of these works have appeared in *Angle, Aufgabe, Big Allis, Crayon, The Germ, Hanging Loose, Inscape, Mirage #4/Period(ical)*, *Oxford Quarterly Review, Parataxis, Shiny, Untitled* and *West Coast Line*; in the anthologies *Noir sur blanc* (Paris: fourbis, 1998—tr. Joseph Guglielmi & Anne Talvaz), and *Sleight of Foot* (London: Reality Street Editions, 1996); and in the chapbook *Facture* (Great Barrington: The Figures, 1999).

Roof Books are distributed by
Small Press Distribution
1341 Seventh Avenue
Berkeley, CA. 94710-1403.
Phone orders: 800-869-7553
spdbooks.org

State of the Arts This book was made possible, in part, by a grant from the New York
State Council on the Arts.

NYSCA

ROOF BOOKS
are published by
The Segue Foundation
303 East 8th Street
New York, NY 10009
segue.org

for John Miles Champion

(June 28, 1938—April 8, 1996)

CONTENTS

THE BEIGE SUPREMATIST

We made some drawings of the volume lengthwise.
There was a typewriter key in the sweat.
What of the resolve that curtains us into a solid trope.
I see him loosen what's moist,
    and acquire a mute pathos.
"That", says Kazimir Malevich, "makes a soap man."
On an island of noise, attach
the sockets to a mucuslike substance.
But what are these wooden pipes on the floor.
Points of beforehand in Deanna's basement.
In the end, though, I came out on the square.
He said it was white and felt cheerful.
Our smooth shapes angled off in flakes of noun breath.
They have the inner beats.
Seems Tim swam off, forming two domes, whose crystals had dislodged.
Put literally the cylinder seems to striate the flicks.
The box that holds it has a burly dynamism.
A sausage-shaped ball roosters about this.
In constructing it, what I say breaks
    into heavy props.
Basic plastic strain exhausts artistic feeling on the roof.

So language, stopping, creates a square.
My sharp eye out, the size is no break, it words the interstices
                       and creates a split.
That chairs be ladders, each chair rescuing a flake.
Chet bakes the fast eye.
It's ridiculous to gargle the lance.
Miss Betty fit the armband, paints, bird mask and a powder nucleus
                    into the stem.
As butter spins so does the powder arm
    against the scape.
Space rebounds from the brink to be gendered.
By the time I get there they have built a new bridge.

The spilt hope of a writing is taken as payment.
She farms the silhouette and I rain.
A gentle person blunts the efficacy of this tool, throwing himself instantly
both back and ahead.
The brief world peels an alto.
Her sister slowly added a radio to the place and watched the redness of
moments but would not participate.

The thought behind it makes a non-balloon on which the feelings
are rung.
Chances are his chair, the sky is the plate, to tune among.
Of course anything can be used to sling shit but the larger structures
are generally more full of it.
They clutch up each around its own excremental figment.
The rabbit has perfected a flag.
A pencil that big will bore the Martians.

It hefts an ego, or a testicle, or both.
He came to, a sky or hole.
Evidently thought was tolerated into runs back past the established wedge
of consensus.
Then an addition dates his grasp, something uncertain sort of parallels
the attributes of technique.
In the heat of something mid-afternoon additions
write up.
Awkward meanings settle beyond the contracts.
I began to smell the set holding sound itself like a stick with the hat on it.
Onlookers are not always sure if the man in the street has
been indoors.
Work flung some distance from a shoe was in
the hills.
The remaining white says put.

PINKING

The buyers keep my hat

on structure   Woods

use skirts lost in the woods   Alone

together   Our teeth in a corner

Cornet   On my lips, the

shape of the word the   Tease,

tone   Airs knit

the pattern's freckle

Decides hangs stuffs

(Patience of the eye to load that

Them, there   Surgically

tenting

the scent of

the treetops   Did

potatoes fugue

Sum rubbing, plainly X

Earlier, liming the portrayalized jinx

Green face

Dilated beer case

two prongs poked thru the paper,

takes the ice cumber, number game

duets soloing, I

log the defect

the woods sore from rain

against the landscape

the indigence of rattling goofs up

our brains   tungsten tears   The cage

momently clogged, blunt pipe   Curved

costs, umbrella footage   A tenor

reaches for the high note

My throat is in my heart, open

mouthed   Ligature of

freshing traits   Hiding tungsten snaps

the oxygen pressure, she hasn't scienced

since yesterday's leap   Tree   Cyclops

The air is cold

We hate the radio

Leaves meanings jogger

Highlinesed map, or woman's sugar

internally stirred by

thoughts, mind shorts   Organic, edible

burners fit tin cups from speckles

throws on the salten pettles

beneath the weeds

burial circumstance

choose life

(bump and goose

chew on mustard seed, heed

what lies otherwise

the leaf of the maker in thrall

faultless no, or undertaken

behind the tree I picture

in my mind's eye

(ill nerve

flaps a heated wire

REMAINDERS/DEW

A woman rinses the card-gloves...
ninth of the fifth
He unlit the fire and undrank a beer
third of the third
Olive green dustpan
third of the second
The summer statue will fog-train the seals
nineteenth of the fourteenth
I don't know—"what issues" jumps up like a spray of water
eighth of the ninth
skylab goldrush is on.
twenty-ninth of the seventh
How I loved to pleat the bright flag!
twenty-eighth of the tenth
Which makes a pencil of the whole spike;
twenty-ninth of the sixth
The tense egg flies off the handle
fifteenth of the twelfth
chicken hand image
twentieth of the fourth
he dangled the phone in a bowl of water
eleventh of the eleventh
The sympathy house is for your feet and the effort is cleaner
twenty-fifth of the thirteenth
To hypnotize a duck with chalk lines drawn from her beak sometimes
level and sometimes forward on a black table.
twenty-fifth of the fifteenth
light kimbrous we can swim
thirty-first of the first
Note that the beaded oar "storms" the reciprocal
eighteenth of the eighth

A crab is bolted onto the shaft

       That priest is enough brick on her gas

     E-shaped with frigid pillars

                Should still is lived corrupts

   An artichoke-proof 1914-18 model

        So tinfoiled that he had pubertized the bulbs

Red small to be

      Supremacy, the balance of

           A +/- lactose calm

  Signs the ever

  Water & wine to form an oblong cut-off

        Or baffle at social what's

    That is, in Hegelian terms, the scarf cigar

  A man is than made

    I think ex-Parisian liver suit or difference

       Perfumes the harder focus

    Road or dog brains rise

     Light is eat

You is in pellet-type pole

 The clearing colour sort of adding the twig

    & I found a kind of digital dried dill

              Stick

   To bust up post-eventual maintenances

       Alloy men panties up you fame

     That days unequal ands

  A fairy's coat or similar irisation

The increased house is

Thus comparing favourably with the impala

Unlikely, seemed, phone

Wilt is envy centimeters

Like a rook religion

I pluck the lint from my omphalos

Wrist is when works ice cold

The smile of evidence

As if you'd swallowed a sort of "doxic" kernel

To on the been

A caliper rayon

Made stucking sounds

In the north in the potato

Gwyllam is in Sardinia photographing bandits

Camisole, goblin

Of things are book

Kipper out the more group

& I vase my meter

Cashiered, muscle-delic

In the gave up

Cuckold broken-winged largely-lettered gadget

Squeezed posture beam

Jewish type of maroons would be "deliberate"

Tit burn

Then perpede furred

On the knees of my heart

Of the spider-god : nervous motorized genius

A matrix for ambient flesh

Dance the fit rind

Since it is made of negated

Boot neither size tired almonds

Testicles she provides

& ownership nine tenths of corset black "E" compose

A socialist's gasp telescope

The eye is the hind part

Soft sandy horses beak to beak

He's yet calculations with cessation

Nuptial flouts pin cab

[self] [o.k.] [Alp]

Each egg wired

Viewy owl

Besides, Aristotle had to verb it

Extremely miniature beige stoop

This deep for its has

Meanwhile, mimicking cravats

They whir against yr face

They get into yr collar & sleeves & shoes

Grounds on the and at

Ban it's night

A foe is decibel

Waves

From can't soap

Maybe revolve moistening papal

With an oily manner pickaxing a wide circle

A tray id I take

Before psychology : cow aisle-ettes

The rhythm as onion wishwonder

Fucking dandy tree soil

Needles this ghost castanet

Keener mathematicians on their condoms

Tactical outpourings prat in a way boom

Lot don't pears

Doublet sense

Another's word rests upon

To has brown

Akin the to flotation

Buckets made of damp

Number shades contain shows in a glass

Stand as camel

Whom whereof there clam

It a then of month

Ambulate, trowel

A pea-tit galosh dresses itself

Nine vowels drop a third vein

To E-flat

& a was airlock

Exchanged by load

Her cups hurting honey

Who unnecks a bowl

OVERLAY

A looped daydream streamed bleak and heatsucking past the windows.
The tram seemed to tangle or lodge in his hair.
A small squid led to a groined arcade.
Could one hurl pens methodically, they sang, to poke
The Cartesian illness. I had to look for these abominably large

Terms in a language and use their absence. I hear she's
Behind her glasses. The tomato in question is the one
Psychoanalysts call ambivalence. Dead? I could feel
Inquisitive goldfish with a rock. A tune popular at the turn. Eye-
Hole mergers. Fan w/ amber stick, ostrich

Blowing on a paper kazoo. Led by a rather sinuous, effeminate Death
In a madrigal for three or four voices. The same week a gas
Bird had lit on the windowsill and watched them.
A true owner need not have possession. A cant concept.
It was drizzling, and I was walking with my head so withdrawn

That the nerves which reflect colour to the brain were strained
Perhaps dreaming of a submarine country. Expressions passed for
    emotions.
They are the work of men. I touched every word I uttered. Cézanne
    shifted
On the pouf. I saw no need to describe. I drew the
Sea wrinkled by a dying mistral. I didn't know, but my hands,

Uneasy bladders, were like panniers carried on either side for
    balance.
Light fell across a bowl. The umbilical tug. A welder
Filled the limits of that world with
Germ plasm. I had, all the same, a nervous stomach which
Fissioned and transferred like an overlay to each retina.

Kimono, or kind of sodality, indulgences remits the temporal
Arrow chalked on the sidewalk. The door.
The room, like a football, blisters the hands that pass it on.
They are skin too. A confusing picture.
Way round cupolas. Fish are sometimes opalescent and sometimes

Their anxiety is the same as my father's. One can drop these dogmas
On their heads. I lengthened pears imperceptibly into needless
    puzzles.
I loved the barren touchlessness of memory.
An exaggerated saddle. Ambiguously a beast.
Freckles fade into the general green. In the distance a name is being

COUNT POINTER COUNT

His mission lay among a few small islands
Looks like heads are blessed with hands
The wipe names, lowering over sentience
And you can reach for it, grab it and pull
Dreams of tangents from the rough circumference

What happens next is locked in pattern
Cut it this way, I don't want chunks
The water dense and gloriously reflective
Kind of lid to drain the scattered mass
Insides waving in the dead light of sunset

Unencumbered except for wings and gnats
So unlaced the outside of the room
I begins with belt and zipper
Sign over door obscured by two
Gauche camels bashed the line of vision across

Blind Spot out at 4.7sec an obvious danger from trap one

FLUID COVER

arms," as

so to

seize (they)

bureaucratic relation

this, the

umbrella of

wealth, presumably

foundation:

this periods

of acclimation

"contribute" to

the lag—(created

exit? and

soldiers who

(non) physical

a night's

private guns

is inimical

quashes the

dossier

a few small

("situation is calm")

soldiers ap-

(its) proper

roads   the same

vein a

bulwark against?

stars—as

chimeras of things

"I can't..."

mould, melts

people in other locales

have not

quenched, wiped-away, different

protest: is

"brandish an attachment

more *concretely*

(who) is

unthrifty, a

even; when

of a "pristine"

retain

& introspection?

I am lucky

even to

"beverage" hence

just illustrates what (...)

(becomes banal)

unit(s)...   felt

unable is

yet—I

soft paths

(bath breathes)

healthy in

"body"

and "mind"

buts how

an internalized

*dis*play

curtains in

"a thousand fugitive details"

surely helps

saves time

above all

one's own

"ossified", &, "unbinding"

mirrors wch

limits aerate

all ears, bombs

, bombard the (a) concept,

attempt to

(ought)

ITSELF

in, end

paint-wise I

...mean...

"porous prisons"

in the ordinary sense

not content

("utterly out of the...")

poor imitations

are, is   vestments

the whatnot

of mind

keeps

boxed in

(a peach nobody)

"with dullside out"

yeast orbits

a lacuna loaf

the vertical

is puffs

pops the

pronoun

seal healing

I hear a

clique we event

(it may be asked)

"any interest"

with deficiency

is seldom

damped down:

substance nudges

news, the

body "make does..."

a greater

condensation

"in the raiment"

limit neighbourhoods

easiest

to document

THE OILCLOTH'S CUFF

The present moss tears
backward but the
true scale wattles off the
clock—green bottles

of Rime which
puff as someone's
nodules pop. Years'
stars flash images

of leveraged gline,
emblem's jars
harden to hold
what you expect

me to leave
out. ("Too nervous,
bulb which whose,
you confuse me

with the reader,
crumpled stillness
with the unattached
map.") Pilots compete

for the sober hue
in a pile. We
step through pink
miasma to the mops.

CLOVIS

Clovis
walked up to the
naked foot—
it must have weighed
about 140.

A sullen boy—
fire hurt him emotionally.
His mind was just inches—
was a cornball
on the edge of a giant
culvert...

I caught a glimpse
of the shakes—
scores of signs
held them at bay
while I shaved.
He said,
"One thing before we leave."
And patted his wallet.

A third cup
under the hood
splashed some water on his face.

I could hear what had to be
in midsentence.

He swore—
like a bizarre
father-son. Stuffing
his comic book into
a large barnlike building.

*   *   *

Bicycle Pete
bumbled on
to Eucalyptus Road
in low—
          Clovis always
opted for
sentiment over truth.

I got into other gigs—
the Sentiment Movement.

The cleats removed!—

Clovis was the "pheasant under glass".

"I have my trough,"
he nodded.
Sentiment encased his blubbery torso.

He sat
on my holster.

The hilly
enclave was
an idiot savant's
antenna.

*   *   *

Clovis lay strewn
on top of the rubble—
he found a
large towel and wiped his
cello.

"Been playing ten years,"
says C,
"The cello is
kind of decadent and
largely elliptical.

Nice pad!"

"It seemed
so...stable,"
Jane blurted.

Clovis understood
her cigarette
for her.

"We ended
and I eyeballed
ass. She shook
plans for the
future."

Jane
found a bench.
Clovis reinforced his hunch.

"You want
to do it?"

Jane passed
and got healthy through
abstinence.

"I don't want to
punch the accelerator
of interesting scents.
Health casts an orange

like a high-priced fruit
into my trunk.

BLAM! BLAM!"

Clovis peddled
rocks
and checked his
health.

His orange
felt steady.

It was rolling strangely.

"Fuck beer!"
Clovis siphons
the inchoate.

"Jane! My cello's
all internal now!"

The edge of it
would put everything
in perspective.

      *   *   *

Passing Bicycle Pete
Hot Rod
smeared some soap
into town. He
juiced
Pete's dollar
and it softened.

Rod dug
Pete's brain
to the repeated drone
Clovis derived
from Chopin's "Heroic
Polonaise"...
On a blanket
an ice cube
looked vapid.

The chickenshit
gave him a
barman's thought
in an ashtray.

The three
cooled
off
as it twisted
under a neon sign.

Two gulps
of horseshit.
Hot Rod
ordered huevos
but Clovis
had dissolved.
Pete burglarized
things that
death rays
numbed.

A small wood.

Bullshit.

Their taste is meagre,
muttered C.

Jane was measuring his words.

Rod
felt his
ball jaundice.

Music more than anything
was a vein in
Jane's forehead. She inhaled
both her shoulders.

"That's...it..."
her voice
was walking ambivalence.

"That orange was
no factory peon.

Rod! Are you still
digging?"
            Pete hid
the choral
porn photos.

Clovis lit
his face
while Jane
hugged the outside
of a glob
and Rod
looked for the answer.

The rest was icing on the
cello and bow.

Clovis filled in
canyons
on the
land
side of the
road...

THE PERSPICACITY OF BLUSHESSE

She snaked her

back up onto

her shoulders

   Drink

up your

Corona there, Mr/

only four stools

and not even

a door,

just a

hand with

a mouth in its

palm. "We're

a *full-service*

shop here

at Coloured

People: may I

bring you

some

complimentary

tea?" Not

like he flat-

out stole

the glasses or

anything,

they just

crawled right

into his

hand. She

ran a thumbnail

over the

bag. "When

shadows

get detached

from people, you

have to

catch

them and

sew them back

on."

RECOGNITION

Stubb: I am inclined to speak of a
       Wordless thinking.
       Who can prepare a blueprint?
       Who is all ears?
       What's the value of this appearance?

Flask: Swelled with content,
       Like a bent pin
       My dark eyes darken.
       The suburbs toss.
       The ends of streets
       Rattle into the letter-box.

Stubb: Spent event, fruitful narration.
       But colour in the eye?
       It gives forth fluid.
       O thy skin, a chamois soft
       As oblivion!

Flask: I burn my head off
       And put on a black pot.
       The husk of silence
       Not the patter and click.
       A steeple pricks up out of a hillock.
       I like it. Mysterious inner needle.

Stubb: This light dates me.
       My steaming flanks wax impersonally.
       Where's the bathroom?
       I...I have a nose which loves.
       I must guard it from the light with fumey air.

Flask: Or dust the muffled force.
        Such grease clogs the arteries
        Where the restaurant was.
        Clever clogs. A permanent cloud.
        Babbled something like hub
        Yelps.

Stubb: Clouds taste metallic.
        Sedate what sounds.
        I was trying to draw
        The kettle, and I saw you.

Flask: What I perceive is this
        Film on life. Or rather,
        Writing presents it.
        Quicksand!
        I smell a rat!
        This seems a good chance to—

Stubb: You smell a what?
        Who put the cart before
        A living symbol?
        Stuff it! A hoarse whisper
        Sustains its propagation.

Flask: Stubb Stubb Stubb Stubb!
        A picture swims before this stove.
        It makes my thoughts boil!
        Listen!

Stubb: Wordless thinking
        Pours out onto the scene
        Unannounced?

Flask: Pours out.

TODAY'S BATH

and lachrymose, a Gazza of the pumps, he
On Thursday, boosted by two months of
the Pennines. Local authorities put the lava-

ham near Bristol where repairs are need-
ural angles show no trace of the attempt to blend
dancing in a bar, somewhere in Europe

can be cloned by taking bulblets from
the big screen. "A big leak," he said
his rheumy eyes can see,

spread on naan bread or chapatis.
Myself and Christopher Bullock used to
squat, moving your knees about 18 inches apart,

the blond model, slowly dis-
includes all of the Beatles recordings.
The other thing, of course, is

buttonholing the curate. I have
posed by recent dry weather, attributed to glob-
es Tory hypocrisy on tobacco and health

talks at police headquarters. In a speech
a different range of futures is traded,
"redbrick" and "Oxbridge" to contrast the 19th

Monroe to tickle the President's fancy
focus. Arnaud Flavole, 72, ate a 5ft 5in
"cell", as approved by all the gurus, and

an aperture in a wall, a mirror or a
brain where physics and chemistry meet the
mess," said a spokesman for Somerset

of these strictures. There is a theory, though, that
is protected by an inner ring
called "lean-burn". The chewed leaves

stress the synergy between book and place
are not prepared to paint double yel-
ly eyesore" is how an old lady

should be exercised more, only perseverance
mate is going to be like. Can we sip
hills, used teargas to disperse them

Clear plastic figures appear to be fucking.

It's fine.

The environment seems watery.

There is a row of sharpened pencil stubs nearby.

The bright cardboard is painful.

The peep-hole leaps wildly.

It suggests a hat.

Something infantilism—roams around.

He is twenty-nine.

The coloured lines do not break.

They function as barriers.

Where the edges meet is like a dissolve.

The results are wide-ranging.

A careening licentiousness is guarded.

This reserve is shared.

It has a milky look.

The coarse blobs become tiny.

A folded-over letter captures the mood.

The breakthrough was in 1959.

It functions pleasurably.

The look is in quotes.

But humour saves the day.

But analysis stops there.

They are handrails, supports, devices of enablement.

The colour is good.

This is perturbing.

An oblong ring sits on the ground.

It has an opulence.

Now this myth is also germane.

The leaves are censorial.

HANG-UP

the doubly inscripted

           retains

     each...of...of...

              "Some

       quilts & our

            slack puck

                    shake, invent

      force. The

              I think...

      cold!

                my size

          crumples

                  (needs salt

    system—we

         ablate

            at

           really

   a gleam to

          (feathers, snorkels

     the clouds FAULTS

              one, shut,

                   for, is, some

      sweet

           ((limELIke))

             , will fog,

up—betw.

summation (i'll

BUZZINGS

ASK

it

puff/swab

shape

& pyramidally "sleeve-wet"

annuls

(no could

scOOp

's like

vibrating specs

what, but

resembling

so (folds) an

brick up

peps to space

as a...is...

snAps

am box still

clay herringbone

THESE LEAF

hewing, caroms

doves, tails...

ifs medicate

FINISHING TOUCHES

The hand

in the

cookie

jar

is pretty

much

out. I was

employing this

thought to

mortgage

the future.

The nod

dis-

members the

tactile

echo of

a solipsistic

gesture. Diffuse

summa-. I

mean, to

provide you

with layers. (Target

fit

mists.) I

was in

the twenty-

four-hour

metaphor, laundering

an intense

& crystalline

hush.

BUFFER

debunking—libidinal

peach, a cheer

out?" There

goes a neutrino just

right. (An

target, still permeates, string

platitudes, sounding

fabric.") Peel

mirth, are subtracted, i.e.

"webs"

of belief—narcissistically

woof, of

talk. One

kidneys; others

bud hard, all horn at the

peppers to the

itch." What

practices—practices

stitch. (Nothing

body.) Wings

are prejudices, that

beat, no

waft of exertion

is almost a pleasure

cobblestones permeated by

my feet. It also follows

him at his word, the

pipes growling

into rivers. A wildly

little gesture

in a mist of dew, is wiped, is wet

again. A dry

eye, but

coagulate, self

the size of the eye's

ear, clear, heels overtaking

use; a

Abbreviated,

green, the sort

of paranoia through

moss. To

by contrast

milieux, potato

couch, crisp

girdle of steel about

sleep. I

to banging one's head on a low

help, buttress

an abortive rill

exemplified by

spotting. (Socially

curious flat

holes, a therapeutic

pssssssssss. Then

"face," ha-ha about

cues. Excuse

VERY STRONG AND VERY WEAK

shape + place = almost individual

*

A divan-like
    mountain of cerebration

*

is skilled in- oblivious

*

The Blue Foetus

    1) boils
    2) kneels down
        a) before a spark
        b) its sister
    3) spits into a pitcher

*

Joan of Arc was
    a hermaphrodite?

Never established. How could it be?
    Elle fut carbonisée.

*

Clarity is
    immobile
    Visual
indifference a
    growth

      *

Too like
one another
to
be days

      *

Each conviction lengthens the sentence

      *

"Backless love,
the city waves me like a napkin in your hand."

      *

avec
la vie

      *

eaten by his
question

      *

    "I do not brood, nor do I
  experiment."
            —Picasso

*

CELLULAR PROSODY

A point is born on a node of the grid.

*

peril eyes in the
    dairy air

*

the June sun
      on the wetted edge
  of downward suction

*

    POE

    there came suddenly to my nostrils
    the equivocal appellation of
    the vessel—the berths of which
    rhymed with the result of such intense
    mental collectedness

*

    TH
    ES
    ES
    HO
    ES

*

WHAT SKY   written after eating

        *

The Detective   less virulence
                    such a pattern

        *

after eyeing the structure I
formed a vapour
of departure and streamed
through

        *

THIS PEN HAS A
LIMITED CAPACITY
OF EITHER 400 WORDS
OR 10 METRES.

        *

"why," in order to better elucidate
                   the "how"

        *

brain, discradled, infinite,
in love with display

        *

the projector's reels
  are the mouse's ears

the rain makes pawprints
on the windshield

*

Apology Clusters

    1) severe abundance
    2) stone fans
    3) colourless walls
    4) bottomless cans

*

(springtime)   bedtime

*

"These are the sentences
    you have to paint."
        —Steve McCaffery

*

No connectives
or interval music
inside
the wave

*

THE is to — — — — as OF is to — — — —.

*

and "it" and "that" are everything

*

"As literature,
　　　　it's fine."
　　　　　　　　—Alfred Jarry

*

English: "not to know what to do with oneself"

French: "not to know what to do with one's skin"

THE SEEDLESS EYEBROW PENCILS

We got hot past the marker in a cloud of

Being still, a "gradual" practice   to set

Open to adversity in the jet stream

Hair cream   floats thru the air

And tried to genie perfume back in

Dust. Becoming a curved bar,

The comb, people's bodies, purses and clothes   losing teeth

Takes the sky in my face out of a tired head.

Lines adopt the refused force and   aim out.

Visualizable roads I mentally concoct

Made still and strong   by the eye

In 1st gear   wobbling past

Coming off corners, wheedling into compartments

Where two lie   buried in their answers   to

Win back somehow, territory lost somehow or other

Running around the waist

With the details of the hip.

Composed of nitrogen   oxygen and trace

A finger along

The rich topsoil all duration

The hoes meanwhile   in rakish light

Make a right turn in the chernozem

Leftly buffeting the air. Just starting up

Purring neutrally

Pouring coffee

Juicing the memory

Of a melody carried rotting in black wax.

Timing is the key,

Schubert is in the alley

Looking for a way out   from behind the mobile comma

Of recent hair on the page nuzzling for attention.

Lines adopt the coloured cloth and

Aim out   food fills   how "good"

An omelet provides notorious gardens

Slice to reveal the darkening air

You brush away with a back of the hand :

Do your arms glow?

Why is twilight narrow :

So :

In a silver bowl,

Not far from the bed at the back of your neck.

Lace fingertips, a fresh wind blowing up dust

This model mind protects

On either side of the glass

Squeezy verbs indent, tapping at windows

Commas like glasses   wine without headlights

The apperception ("splash") to carry in the head

"Little scuffy motors"

Mar

Shalling the dirt bikes of the intellect

Thru the fog of a picture-perfect beach.

"Splash"   the scenery blisters at 70mph

Pirates grab at things

In the throes of a "rash" of reflections

Bald sky oiling the ground   the waves bending

Report to the doctor

With a stiff upper lip. Fog

Detains the miniscule diamonds

Or, clouds evoke grey

From this perspective, providing alleys

Blocked by a fulminating X   the doctor

Takes out his flashlight.   Lamplight displays gear

Lemon wedges thriving in moonlight   speech and glue

Soaked in fog

Dipped in a disguise   of day before night

Whatever time   feathering rivulets

The bed is eating figs under the coverlet

Waves receding under the Cadillac of bays.

Striking a pose when the wind drops a phrase

The sun attacks, runs from associations

Toward abbreviations, i.e.   a glass of water, the ocean

"Dirt bikes marshalling"

My sense of duration   which is short   remains skeptical

I could sit and be jealous over distinctions

Fluffed-up seats are trained to attention

Mud hens hoist themselves up to the level, waves rotund,

A crystalline

Postcard,   the seedless eyebrow pencils

Charge with a static that binds as their heads are pressed

SKY

Cramped about

my

head

admits happy

tokens

beyond what

air of

solitude lies

under this

cloud

blanket of

flat regard

wasting by

time

mornings float

standard reductions

safe bets

buckled or

sewn across

lightening

frowns

clutch

from fanned

tenderness to

my place

I

get up

breeze through

off-white

out the

detail

again these

border mists

thoughts pass

my body

line-like

gives directions

molts lightly

aches

THE TWO HOLE EXPERIMENT

Though bland not watery but stickily present

Mauves worn against lopsided hope
as garlic to the martyr's sniff

Zeros out of scale
and pockets
of warmth under the why-for

Dispersals
and recombinative pleasures
swelling turntypes
and two-armed insertions

All that had plunged under language
was viscous
tired of proof
mating with the hole
beneath an expression of action

Not a care
but the case of
dig for clues
outdistance reason and glow
cover the windows
with transparent squares

Scrutinized upon
emerging
looking down upon
mimetic borders
how many
enough to form the work
the unrhyming

That which
leaks from its edge
not pervasive
that which
that held up a scented truck
as foreground
against the shapeless present
not with

Cornering
each implement
and fasting
the mind's plunge
is an error in space
pressed into thin wax
with no meat for silence
like the lathed and battered
finally erect

The wink
and attentions
of buildings
a glaze of experience
to boil the present
to costume the towers in steam
my face reflects the light
to give words their names
a shaft nudges
the profile of dust out of place

POEM

Candour disposes the lustre

tinctures for what chance

the person's mount or invisible tailpiece

free brochurettes impressing the indefinite fold

cuffed hands spool to avert

is pierced or will burst

sewed

knees together partly knot

or stick that lies therein whetting

hearts to fetter the regret

ankle or nebulous

seeds or principles robot capsizing

for the win of parked

lamps

retract the valence

of the miniature headset of the transitive

froth dislocated the tangible heel of the symboliser

I would say along

eyes toward verisimilitude

the lovely paper of my ghost

YELLOW SUGAR

metre, "as stone"

fed through the level, but

claims, do well

as support for and

techniques. Each

bird or bush" which display a

is interpretable. Similarly,

through. Such reaching

is compelled — even

fantastical. Needless to say, both

reader no hold, nor have they the

"Stetson". This

coherence, relation even

year-round strawberries

yellow wooden ones

thematic, with minor patterns

implied by the

least emendation. Let us take one

texture and movement (the acme

which meaning is inferred, as in

frozen. Again, no, for it eludes

any attempt to

give them. The image does not prove

gets too much

between limitations on

scale, is to be the very backbone of the

legs." This extension

or else a point

precluded. So that

seemingly detached

it could never

kind leads, if it is bent

ROOF BOOKS

- Andrews, Bruce. **EX WHY ZEE.** 112p. $10.95.
- Andrews, Bruce. **Getting Ready To Have Been Frightened.** 116p. $7.50.
- Benson, Steve. **Blue Book.** Copub. with The Figures. 250p. $12.50
- Bernstein, Charles. **Islets/Irritations.** 112p. $9.95.
- Bernstein, Charles (editor). **The Politics of Poetic Form.** 246p. $12.95; cloth $21.95.
- Brossard, Nicole. **Picture Theory.** 188p. $11.95.
- Champion, Miles. **Three Bell Zero.** 72p. $10.95.
- Child, Abigail. **Scatter Matrix.** 79p. $9.95.
- Davies, Alan. **Active 24 Hours.** 100p. $5.
- Davies, Alan. **Signage.** 184p. $11.
- Davies, Alan. **Rave.** 64p. $7.95.
- Day, Jean. **A Young Recruit.** 58p. $6.
- Di Palma, Ray. **Motion of the Cypher.** 112p. $10.95.
- Di Palma, Ray. **Raik.** 100p. $9.95.
- Doris, Stacy. **Kildare.** 104p. $9.95.
- Dreyer, Lynne. **The White Museum.** 80p. $6.
- Edwards, Ken. **Good Science.** 80p. $9.95.
- Eigner, Larry. **Areas Lights Heights.** 182p. $12, $22 (cloth).
- Gizzi, Michael. **Continental Harmonies.** 92p. $8.95.
- Gottlieb, Michael. **Ninety-Six Tears.** 88p. $5.
- Gottlieb, Michael. **Gorgeous Plunge.** 96p. $11.95.
- Greenwald, Ted. **Jumping the Line.** 120p. $12.95.
- Grenier, Robert. **A Day at the Beach.** 80p. $6.
- Grosman, Ernesto. **The XUL Reader: An Anthology of Argentine Poetry (1981–1996).** 167p. $14.95.
- Hills, Henry. **Making Money.** 72p. $7.50. VHS videotape $24.95. Book & tape $29.95.
- Huang Yunte. **SHI: A Radical Reading of Chinese Poetry.** 76p. $9.95
- Hunt, Erica. **Local History.** 80 p. $9.95.
- Kuszai, Joel (editor) **poetics@**, 192 p. $13.95.
- Inman, P. **Criss Cross.** 64 p. $7.95.
- Inman, P. **Red Shift.** 64p. $6.
- Lazer, Hank. **Doublespace.** 192 p. $12.
- Lazer, Hank. **Doublespace.** 192 p. $12.
- Levy, Andrew. **Paper Head Last Lyrics.** 112 p. $11.95.
- Mac Low, Jackson. **Representative Works: 1938–1985.** 360p. $12.95, $18.95 (cloth).
- Mac Low, Jackson. **Twenties.** 112p. $8.95.
- Moriarty, Laura. **Rondeaux.** 107p. $8.
- Neilson, Melanie. **Civil Noir.** 96p. $8.95.
- Pearson, Ted. **Planetary Gear.** 72p. $8.95.
- Perelman, Bob. **Virtual Reality.** 80p. $9.95.
- Perelman, Bob. **The Future of Memory.** 120p. $14.95.
- Piombino, Nick, **The Boundary of Blur.** 128p. $13.95.
- Raworth, Tom. **Clean & Will-Lit.** 106p. $10.95.

❏ Robinson, Kit. **Balance Sheet.** 112p. $11.95.
❏ Robinson, Kit. **Democracy Boulevard.** 104p. $9.95.
❏ Robinson, Kit. **Ice Cubes.** 96p. $6.
❏ Scalapino, Leslie. **Objects in the Terrifying Tense Longing from Taking Place.** 88p. $9.95.
❏ Seaton, Peter. **The Son Master.** 64p. $5.
❏ Sherry, James. **Popular Fiction.** 84p. $6.
❏ Silliman, Ron. **The New Sentence.** 200p. $10.
❏ Silliman, Ron. **N/O.** 112p. $10.95.
❏ Smith, Rod. **Protective Immediacy.** 96p. $9.95
❏ Stephans, Brian Kim. **Free Space Comix.**
❏ Templeton, Fiona. **Cells of Release.** 128p. with photographs. $13.95.
❏ Templeton, Fiona. **YOU—The City.** 150p. $11.95.
❏ Ward, Diane. **Human Ceiling.** 80p. $8.95.
❏ Ward, Diane. **Relation.** 64p. $7.50.
❏ Watten, Barrett. **Progress.** 122p. $7.50.
❏ Weiner, Hannah. **We Speak Silent.** 76 p. $9.95
❏ Yasusada, Araki. **Doubled Flowering: From the Notebooks of Araki Yasusada.** 272p. $14.95.

Roof Books are distributed by
SMALL PRESS DISTRIBUTION
1341 Seventh Avenue, Berkeley, CA. 94710-1403.
Phone orders: 800-869-7553
spdbooks.org

ROOF BOOKS
are published by
Segue Foundation, 303 East 8th Street, New York, NY 10009
Visit our website at **segue.org**